Changing Lives Through

VIRTUAL REALITY

Other titles in *The Tech Effect* series include:

The Tech
EFFECT

Changing Lives Through
VIRTUAL REALITY

James Roland

ReferencePoint
Press

San Diego, CA

© 2021 ReferencePoint Press, Inc.
Printed in the United States

For more information, contact:
ReferencePoint Press, Inc.
PO Box 27779
San Diego, CA 92198
www.ReferencePointPress.com

LIBRARY OF CONGRESS CATALOGING-IN-PUBLICATION DATA

Names: Roland, James, author.
Title: Changing lives through virtual reality / by James Roland.
Description: San Diego, CA : ReferencePoint Press, [2021] | Series: The
   tech effect | Includes bibliographical references and index.
Identifiers: LCCN 2020002100 (print) | LCCN 2020002101 (ebook) | ISBN
   9781682828496 (library binding) | ISBN 9781682828502 (ebook)
Subjects: LCSH: Virtual reality--Social aspects--Juvenile literature.
Classification: LCC HM851 .R6635 2021 (print) | LCC HM851 (ebook) | DDC
   006.8--dc23
LC record available at https://lccn.loc.gov/2020002100
LC ebook record available at https://lccn.loc.gov/2020002101

CONTENTS

Virtual Reality Opens Doors to Real and Unreal Worlds

A pod of massive humpback whales swims by, the calves playing while the older whales lead the annual migration from Antarctica to the warmer waters of the Pacific Ocean. To be in the middle of this natural wonder would be thrilling yet dangerous. But to students wearing a virtual reality (VR) headset and enjoying Immotion's *Swimming with Humpbacks* experience, the mighty pectoral fins of these endangered mammals can seem inches away, even though the students have not left the safety of their classrooms on dry land.

virtual
Simulated; in this case, created by computer software to appear as though it physically exists

Studying whales by swimming alongside them virtually is one of countless ways VR is changing the way people learn. However, this technology is also having a huge impact on how people play, shop, do business, and just live their lives today. "We're going to see VR shape industries over the next few years in ways we haven't even thought about yet—it's an incredible time to be a part of it all,"[1] says VR developer Liv Erickson.

For example, shoppers in India were among the first consumers to find Amazon VR kiosks at their local malls. Individuals could place a VR headset on and take a fun balloon ride into a town populated with products available through Amazon Prime. Akshay Sahi, head of Amazon Prime in India, told Quartz:

> How do you discover 200-plus products that are not in the market yet? Last year, customers told us "we loved the stuff when we got it but we were wary while buying it since it was not something we'd ever seen. So now with VR, people can see the products in their true form factor. They can see how a microwave is going to look on a countertop and how a dress looks on a model. You can see jewelry up close and observe it in great detail.[2]

Students prepare for a virtual reality experience while seated in their classroom.

How VR Works

Just as the internet connects people and information in ways never imagined, VR is providing experiences that are only limited by the imagination and the rapidly changing technology that computer scientists, engineers, and artists are using every day to expand the virtual world. To put a very complicated concept simply, VR uses computer technology to create a simulated, 3-D environment that users can explore and manipulate as though they were in that world. VR requires a headset and programs that are downloaded as apps, in the same way games or social media platforms are downloaded onto a smartphone. VR's cousin, augmented reality (AR), is already common on smart devices, allowing users to interact with virtual images projected onto their real-world environment. It is the technology behind, for example, *Pokémon Go* and Snapchat filters.

augment
Make greater or more intense

Much of the VR and AR technology is used for entertainment or to provide nearly impossible experiences, like swimming with whales or exploring the surface of Mars. And for anyone who has already donned a VR headset to battle bad guys in a video game or watch VR movies, virtual reality seems ideally suited for entertainment. With traditional screen-based media, a turn of the head means the action goes out of sight. But with the all-encompassing environments of VR, looking up, down, or to the side just provides a new angle on the never-ending story or game experience. But beyond creating novelty experiences, VR is changing lives in more serious and practical ways too.

VR technology can let car shoppers take a realistic test drive in a custom-designed vehicle. In the medical field, it allows surgeons to get a preview of a complicated cardiac operation by taking a virtual tour of the patient's heart. VR is also helping patients cope with pain and anxiety. It provides therapists with a new tool to assist individuals in confronting phobias and other mental or physical challenges.

Creating Change

It may seem odd to think of developments in a virtual, "unreal" world changing the lives of people in the real world, but that is exactly what is happening every day. Surgeons, engineers, shoppers, and students are peering into VR headsets as the future comes into focus today. "More innovation will be required before VR becomes the huge success that it can be," says Jesse Joudrey, chief executive officer (CEO) of VRChat. "But already we're seeing the potential to be influential in every industry including education, transportation, architecture, medicine and a number of entertainment industries. . . . It's no longer a question of whether VR will change them, but how much change it will create."[3]

CHAPTER ONE

Entertainment

Long before computer-generated images found their way into games and movies, the concept of VR had a firm place in popular entertainment. Massive 360-degree panoramic paintings depicting cityscapes and historic battles drew big crowds in the 1800s. During the same era there emerged handheld stereoscopic viewers that used photographic tricks to create some of the first 3-D images ever seen. Stereoscopic films that relied on dual projectors to create moving 3-D images emerged in the early 1920s, but movie studios were more interested in improving the quality of standard 2-D films and adding sound to motion pictures than innovating 3-D. Interest in 3-D movies waned until the 1950s, when 3-D became a popular gimmick, mostly used in horror films like *House of Wax* or low-budget science fiction movies such as *Robot Monster*. In the decades that followed, revolutionary advances in computer technology brought VR to where it is today.

In the 1980s, when the term *virtual reality* was coined and the worlds of VR began to look more like their current renderings, VR technology remained primarily planted in the realm of entertainment. VR applications in medicine, education, engineering, and other fields were either nonexistent or were only vague ideas of engineers, scientists, and especially imaginative VR pioneers.

Video games, movies, theme park rides, and other forms of entertainment continue to be the forces that drive innovation in VR and the ways most people in the general public still think of and use VR technology. And video games continue to be the center of that VR universe. "Games are still the primary driver of the industry, with 59 percent of developers' current or potential VR and AR projects falling in the gaming space,"[4] writes Peter Rubin for *Wired*.

Video Games: The Heart of VR Innovation

Players feel the sensation of soaring through the clouds, mysterious high-tech aircraft firing earsplitting rockets at them from everywhere they look. They fire back with powerful energy pulses and hope that their Iron Man armor holds up. After years of watching Marvel's Iron Man battle the bad guys on the big screen, audiences can don Tony Stark's iconic Iron Man suit—at least a virtual one—in Marvel's *Iron Man VR* game for the Sony PlayStation. "It's the perfect marriage of technology and character, a fusion of human and machine, just as Tony himself,"[5] says Bill Rosemann with Marvel Games.

fusion
The joining of two or more separate items

Video games like *Iron Man VR*, the award-winning space adventure *No Man's Sky*, and the VR version of the classic *Skyrim* place users in the middle of superhero clashes, sword-and-sorcery adventures, modern-day battlefields, haunted houses, outer space explorations, and other environments. These novel experiences are competing with traditional games for the attention of players looking for new fun and thrills. The VR industry website VRROOM says immersion is what sets VR games apart:

> The feeling of being placed in a virtual gaming world, where when you look to your left then look to your right, when all you can see and all you can feel is that virtual world . . . that's immersion. Being allowed to interact with your hands by picking up virtual objects within the game . . . that's immersion. Immersion is the difference maker in what virtual reality can truly offer the gamer.[6]

And though the early generations of VR video games were often limited in scope—players could usually complete all the levels within a few hours—the potential for an exciting future in immersive games was obvious from the outset. The attraction is not just the opportunity to feel surrounded by a new environment but the interaction with characters in ways that flat-screen video games cannot provide. VR puts players alongside 3-D characters so that the users can more deeply identify with these characters and not just watch them from a distance.

VR games are also just starting to bring their unique immersive qualities and

immersive
Relating to a computer-generated 3-D environment that appears to surround a person

character interactions to the world of massive multiplayer online role-playing games, in which players from anywhere can come together via the internet to compete and share adventures.

"The combination of presence and empathy has the ability to help socially connect people in new ways, help people experience fantastical and real places in new ways, and open up new ways of looking at and experiencing play, content, live experiences and more," says Jeff Pobst, CEO of Hidden Path Entertainment, makers of the popular VR game *Raccoon Lagoon*. "That sounds pretty exciting to me."[7]

The Comfort Challenge

While no one disputes VR's potential as a game-changing innovation, one thing that may slow down its popularity is the headset itself. Many people find a headset uncomfortable to wear for long periods. Pobst says:

> There is the inherent friction for many people around putting a large headset onto their head, and the miniaturization of headsets over time will likely be one of the largest technological advances that will help reduce the difficulties for players and help grow adoption of VR. Allowing more and more people the opportunity to comfortably and easily give VR a try will make a big impact.[8]

Another concern for VR game developers is that the headset technology and game images trigger nausea and dizziness in some users. VR headsets continue to be a one-size-fits-all piece of equipment, yet users have differences that can keep them from fully enjoying VR games. Jason Kingsley, cofounder of the British game company Rebellion, makers of the VR version of the classic tank game *Battlezone*, says:

How headsets display the virtual world to you is always a challenge, and people's biology differs a lot. People see things differently, have different vision in different eyes, are nearsighted or farsighted, have issues with motion sickness, and so on. There are all sorts of components that go into creating a comfortable illusion of being elsewhere. That's a major area that requires continued innovation.[9]

Along with finding ways to make VR work for all types of users, developers are also working to fine-tune the graphics so that the detail and action live up to the imaginative ideas of game designers. The resolution of the castles, aliens, and other VR elements needs to catch up to the stories, settings, and characters finding their way into VR headsets everywhere. "I've demoed VR to dozens of first-timers, and after the initial 'wow factor' wears off, they often ask why the world is so blurry,"[10] says Ryan Payton, founder and designer at Camouflaj, a VR production studio.

Arcades

VR games are not confined to headsets and game consoles at home. For bigger thrills and spills or to enjoy VR experiences that require more than a headset and handheld game controllers, users are venturing out to gaming arcades that are making room for the latest in high-tech fun.

Users who step onto the tilting platform of the Extreme Machine simulator at any of the Dave & Buster's arcade restaurants, for instance, can strap on a VR headset, grab hold of the handlebar in front of them for balance, and take virtual rides on roller coasters, waterfall-diving kayaks, prehistoric flying dinosaurs, snowboards, and much more. These kinds of immersive experiences add to their simulated worlds by moving users up, down, and all around in sync with the action on the screen—even blowing air in moments when the wind picks up on-screen.

Many arcades have one or a few such VR games, but the nature of VR-focused arcades is moving beyond the traditional

Virtual Violins

While movies and games are natural fits for VR's immersive qualities, other art forms are using VR to attract fans. Symphony aficionados, for example, may be able to feel like they are joining the string section of their favorite orchestra. Even if viewers have never mastered the violin or the cello, the VR experience can put users onstage with the orchestra. "Imagine being in . . . your local symphony," says Foo Conner, CEO of the digital media platform Jekko. "Virtual reality places you there. Not mono, not stereo, but hundreds of movable points of sound. Want to hear that violin? Move closer."

The Los Angeles Philharmonic led with this idea in recent years with its Van Beethoven project. A van equipped with VR equipment travels to museums, arts festivals, and other locations, allowing users to put on a headset and feel like they are onstage with the musicians performing Beethoven's Fifth Symphony. The goal? Use new technology to create new fans. "We tried to have it emulate real life as much as possible," says Pietro Gagliano, executive director of Secret Location, the digital studio that worked on the project. For example, users can pick up subtle shifts in sound if they turn their heads to different parts of the virtual auditorium. And for Hyekyung Shin, an early user of the L.A. Symphony's VR experience, the opportunity to feel she was among the musicians gave her a whole new perspective on classical music. "I liked being able to make eye contact with the conductor," she says.

Quoted in *Arkenea* (blog), "16 Experts Predict the Future of Virtual Reality," 2016. https://arkenea.com.

Quoted in David Ng, "L.A. Philharmonic's Van Beethoven Takes Virtual Reality for a Classical Spin," *Los Angeles Times*, September 24, 2015. www.latimes.com.

game center. That is because there is not much difference between VR games at home and what many arcades offer. To get people out of their homes to play VR games, developers are creating free-roam experiences, in which teams of players can put on their headsets, fan out across a wide-open arena, and do battle with zombies, aliens, killer robots, and other enemies. It is like a paintball park with a real high-tech twist . . . and fewer bruises.

One example of a growing free-roam VR experience is Zero Latency, a chain of location-based VR venues in more than a dozen countries. Location-based VR unites the VR world with a real-world location that is commonly filled with items that players can interact with. The items are translated by camera into the VR environment, so a user picking up a book in a specially designed gaming room will see a book in the VR world. In the real-world that book might be a dictionary, but in the VR environment it might appear to be a wizard's tome of magical spells. "People are looking for differentiated, exciting experiences on their night out, on birthday parties, and corporate events," says Doug Griffin, head of Nomadic, a location-based VR company. "People want to get together. People want to physically engage with one another and do something really unique. By creating these fantastic worlds, the most immersive experiences on the planet, I think we deliver something that they can't get elsewhere."[11]

Theme Parks

And just as arcades are retrofitting their game rooms to make them VR-friendly and location-based VR venues are springing up around the globe, theme parks are boosting their VR presence too. Some VR-only theme parks are emerging, and some traditional theme parks that used to draw crowds by building taller and faster roller coasters and waterslides are now adding VR and AR experiences to their existing rides.

The Iron Dragon in Cedar Point, Ohio, opened as a roller coaster with seats suspended from an overhead track, swinging riders out and back for nearly three minutes of screaming, laughing fun. But with the addition of some wild VR elements in recent years, Iron Dragon riders now face attacking ogres and orcs as they fly through a fairy-tale village aboard seats that appear to the riders to look and act like their very own dragons. Similar retrofits are being done in other theme parks. For example, with the help of VR technology, a waterslide at a park in Germany transformed into a crazy canoe ride down an erupting volcano.

Visitors to Hong Kong's Ocean Park ride the VR Mine Train. Adding VR to a traditional ride takes a rider's experience to a whole new level.

But having to shoehorn VR experiences onto existing rides and attractions limits what developers can create. To free up the imaginations of creative VR developers and designers, theme park owners have recently started building separate parks specifically as VR and AR experiences. "The advantages of going VR for theme parks are multiple," says Malcolm Burt, a researcher who studies the entertainment and business sides of theme parks and other amusement attractions. "It's relatively easy to trick the brain into thinking it's somewhere else, and it's substantially cheaper to create a VR attraction than a traditional coaster or flat ride. These experiences can also be updated quickly: Think of a Christmas or Halloween-themed version of an existing offering."[12]

David Schaefer, vice president of the theme park attraction designer Falcon's Creative Group, says that designing a VR experience or ride from the outset allows designers to innovate and push boundaries. The only limits are the existing VR technology and the budget. "VR has percolated enough that we're starting

To VR or Not to VR

Drawing new fans to another legendary figure of the arts—William Shakespeare—is also the goal of *Hamlet 360: Thy Father's Spirit*, an hour-long VR adaptation of the classic play produced by the Commonwealth Shakespeare Company of Massachusetts. The person who wears the headset becomes the mist-shrouded ghost of Hamlet's father, a key character in the play who exchanges dialogue with real actors and can appear to move about the stage, seeing curtains, fellow performers, props, and the audience. Steve Maler, director of the company, says:

> At Commonwealth Shakespeare Company, our mission, really, is to democratize Shakespeare. You know, we wanted to use this extraordinary technology to really scale the mission that we have on the Boston Common every summer, which is bringing excellent Shakespeare to everyone. We serve about 50,000 people in the summer, but we thought it would be quite amazing to be able to really serve the world.

Maler wants *Hamlet 360* and future such productions to become staples in high schools, retirement communities, and every place in which seeing Shakespeare performed live is not a realistic option for the people living there. "I think it's very hard to bring excellent productions of Shakespeare into high schools to animate the classroom with this kind of material," he says. "So, for me, the ability to bring these performances, portable, into a classroom is profound. And I think that is something that I hope will inspire people to love literature, to love Shakespeare, and yes, to love live theater."

Quoted in Folger Shakespeare Library, "*Hamlet 360*: Virtual Reality Shakespeare," April 16, 2019. www.folger.edu.

to see attractions that are purpose-built," Schaefer says, adding that his company is working on projects that will better showcase the promise of the technology. "VR as a bespoke, custom, new attraction: That's where we will start to see advances. By building it from the ground up, we will unshackle designers."[13]

Immersed in the Movies

Just as VR rides and games are surrounding people with new stories and adventures, so too are movies inviting audiences to share experiences alongside the characters on film. Though big-budget VR movies are still on the horizon, filmmakers around the world are making smaller, shorter, but still immersive 3-D movies.

The Venice Film Festival, one of the oldest and most respected film festivals in the world, started a VR competition alongside the traditional categories for feature films and smaller, experimental films. Entries in recent years have included animated science fiction shorts, documentaries about subjects ranging from the bombing of Ireland in World War II to breast cancer treatment, and an artistic journey across the lunar landscape called *To the Moon*.

bespoke
Made for a specific user

Unlike a traditional 3-D film, in which every audience member sees the scenes and experiences the effects in the exact same way, VR movies allow each viewer the chance to watch the action from a different perspective or to turn away from the main action and focus on what is happening elsewhere in the scene. A person can watch the same VR movie countless times and experience it a little differently each time, all with a turn of the head. *To the Moon* director Hsin-Chien Huang says:

> The way we're using this technology allows you to be free and that's the biggest thing about VR that I love: It's that you are not presented with a work of art as is that can't change, but you walk into it, fly into it, you become it. This is what we want people to do. We want them to walk into works of art and wander around inside them and see what they can see. I have a secret goal, which is that people feel free and they're not trapped by their minds.[14]

Filmmakers have been edging closer to VR-style filmmaking since the 1950s with 3-D movies that audiences enjoyed with special plastic glasses. The usual 3-D offerings were low-budget horror or science fiction movies, in which the 3-D elements were more of a gimmick than a way to draw audiences into the stories. IMAX took 3-D films to the next levels with Dolby sound, stadium seating, and huge curved screens that wrapped partially around the audience. Most big-budget adventure movies these days are presented in IMAX as well as traditional versions.

IMAX ride film theaters in theme parks now offer the same high-tech detail as regular IMAX theaters but place audiences on seats mounted on a moving platform or on seats that move or shake on a fixed platform. The movement of the seats or plat-

3-D movies, which are viewed through special plastic glasses, have been around since the 1950s.

form are synced to the projecting equipment so the motion will be timed to the appropriate action in the film every time. When the hero's spaceship dives and swerves in pursuing the villain across the galaxy, audience members dive and swerve along with it. It is a different kind of immersive experience, but the moving seats approach is usually limited to short films, like Disneyland's *Millennium Falcon: Smuggler's Run* attraction, which lasts about fifteen minutes.

VR is rapidly changing game-playing and moviegoing experiences. As players and audiences demand better technology, more realistic effects, and stories and experiences that can best be enjoyed in VR, the creative people behind VR entertainment must be ready to meet those demands. Storytellers, game designers, and others in the industry have glimpsed what is possible with VR and are ready to make real the unreal worlds of their imaginations. As Michel Reilhac, cocurator of the Venice Film Festival's VR program says, "If cinema is the art of playing with time, VR is the art of playing with both time and space. And we are just beginning to understand what that means."[15]

CHAPTER TWO

Health and Medicine

A medical school student holds surgical tools in each hand as he looks down at a patient on an operating table. But to anyone else in the room, it is clear no one is in front of this future surgeon. In addition to scrubs and a surgical mask, Brett Chapa also wears a VR headset and handles electronic tools that are designed to provide realistic feedback to their users. A virtual scalpel makes an incision, and Chapa feels the resistance of skin and tissue slowly giving way to reach the bones of a virtual patient.

anatomy
The scientific study of the body and the way its parts are arranged

"VR is a perfect introduction to anatomy, as it allows the student to make mistakes often," Chapa says. "Mistakes are an essential part of education."[16] The great advantage of VR in training doctors is that virtual patients can suffer countless errors—unlike patients in the real world. VR bodies can return to their original state after an anatomy lesson or virtual surgery, ready for the next medical student.

Before physicians and psychologists start treating people in need, they are learning their crafts with the help of VR. It is being used around the world to train future doctors and provide current health care providers with the latest tools to diagnose and treat conditions such as brain tumors and blocked arteries. Augmented reality, in which virtual elements are presented in a real-world environment, has recently proved to be a promising technology in training doctors and nurses to diagnose wounds and learn about new medical instruments and procedures.

Training Tools

Victims of an underground subway disaster need help. Smoke and cries for help fill the air. First responders arrive at the scene to start triage—a quick evaluation of those who are hurt to determine which injuries are the most serious and in need of immediate

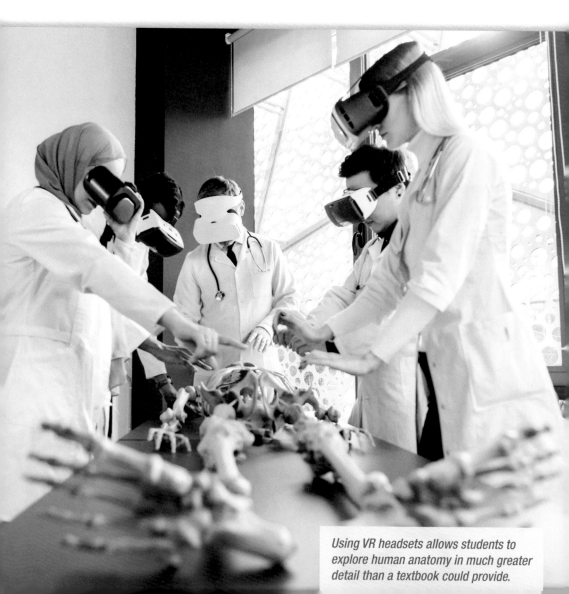

Using VR headsets allows students to explore human anatomy in much greater detail than a textbook could provide.

care. It is an awful scene that calls for highly trained emergency medical technicians (EMTs), paramedics, and doctors.

Thankfully, though, the victims in this scenario are computer generated. Even the equipment in the medical bag used by the responders exists only in the VR simulation developed at the Ohio State University College of Medicine. Trainees, including EMTs and medical students, don VR headsets to find themselves in a darkened tunnel and surrounded by torn metal, broken glass, and wounded passengers of all ages.

This VR simulation is a big step up from previous simulations that included mannequins and actors pretending to be injured. The types of injury and the numbers of injured can be adjusted to match the experience and training of the people using the system. A medical student or EMT without much experience might encounter three or four victims. "A paramedic, an EMT, first responder who needs to be really—and probably already is—pretty skilled at this, we would create a much more difficult scene," says Douglas Danforth, academic program director at the Ohio State University College of Medicine. "And we're going to create it so that you can level up if you treat everybody correctly."[17]

The use of virtual accident victims and virtual patients is growing quickly, especially at medical schools around the world, as VR becomes an invaluable training tool for students. Unlike cadavers, which have a limited window of time during which they are safe and useful, VR patients can present countless symptoms and conditions to future physicians, nurses, paramedics, and other health care providers. The computer-generated individuals can, for instance, respond to their care, letting medical students and experienced doctors see whether their virtual patients are improving or getting worse. For example, the VR patient's skin color changes to denote a worsening of the patient's condition, while a virtual blood pressure monitor and other equipment emit

cadaver
A human corpse, often used to teach anatomy to medical students

Seeing the World Through Older Eyes

Among VR's many applications in health care, some of the most compelling are those programs that help medical students, doctors, and other providers get a better sense of what their patients are experiencing. One virtual world, developed with the assistance of the Alzheimer's Association, lets users experience some of the same confusing observations and feelings as an older person with dementia.

"I'm often asked—what does it feel like to have dementia? These virtual reality modules can help others experience that," says Neelum Aggarwal, a professor at Rush University Medical Center in Chicago. "For the students, it's a good check to see if they have empathy for their patients and are aware of any biases they may have towards people with dementia."

While wearing the headset, users enter the virtual world of Beatriz, an older Latina woman progressing from early dementia to Alzheimer's disease dementia. The stages are presented as short, immersive films that illustrate the struggles of shopping in a grocery store and other everyday activities.

"Technology like this may be useful in expanding awareness about what it is like to have Alzheimer's disease dementia," says Beth Kallmyer, vice president of care and support for the Alzheimer's Association.

Quoted in Alzheimer's Association, "Technology May Improve Understanding and Empathy for Older Adults," July 23, 2018. www.alz.org.

signals that sound like alarms. "Those are all cues to us that okay, I have to do this now or else I'm going to be in trouble," says Joshua Sherman, a pediatric emergency medicine specialist at Children's Hospital Los Angeles. "And when you make that action, you watch it change and that gives you positive reinforcement that you did the correct thing, or the incorrect thing, if the situation gets worse. VR is amazing for that."[18]

There are, however, limitations in training on VR patients. Despite their sophisticated responses and detailed anatomy, they cannot represent the range of people and body types doctors encounter every day. "Every patient is going to be different, so you're not always going to have this perfect 3D model," says Josh Pahang, a medical student at Washington State University. "That's one big limitation."[19]

VR and Brain Health

Real-world limitations are plentiful when it comes to diagnosing and treating brain-related illnesses. Doctors often must rely on outward symptoms because getting to explore a living person's brain is not always practical. For example, getting lost is a common early symptom of Alzheimer's disease. A person's internal navigation system tracks where the person has been, where he

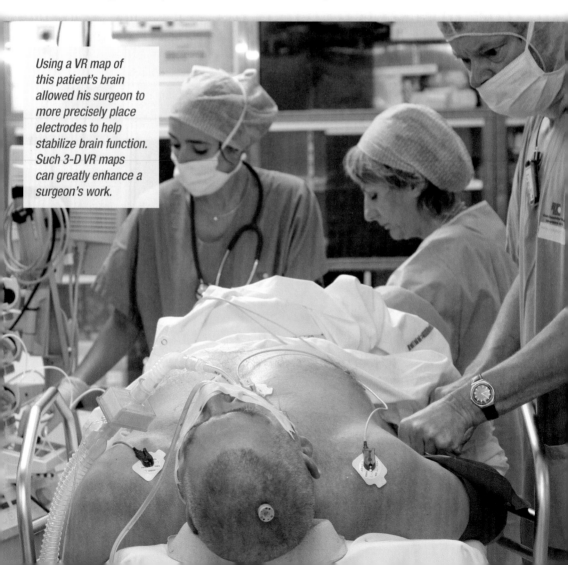

Using a VR map of this patient's brain allowed his surgeon to more precisely place electrodes to help stabilize brain function. Such 3-D VR maps can greatly enhance a surgeon's work.

or she is, and how to find the next destination. The part of the brain that helps manage that navigation process is the entorhinal (behind the nose) cortex, and it is also one of the first parts of the brain harmed by Alzheimer's disease.

Typically, a doctor may give someone suspected of Alzheimer's disease a series of tests to evaluate thinking skills, memory, personality changes, and other traits that are usually affected by the condition. But in recent years, scientists have developed a VR experience that may diagnose the disease more accurately by checking for navigation difficulties.

Wearing a VR headset, patients walk through a simulated environment that tests their navigation skills. Successful completion of the test depends on a healthy entorhinal cortex. But difficulty with navigation suggests a greater likelihood of poor entorhinal cortex function and possibly Alzheimer's disease. "These results suggest a VR test of navigation may be better at identifying early Alzheimer's disease than tests we use at present in clinic and in research studies,"[20] says researcher Dennis Chan of the University of Cambridge.

Other brain and nervous system problems can be just as difficult to decipher as Alzheimer's disease. A VR program developed at the Ottawa Hospital in Canada is being used to map the brain of a person with Parkinson's disease and allow a neurosurgeon to plan the placement of electrodes during deep brain stimulation. Parkinson's is a neuromuscular disease caused by abnormal levels of certain brain chemicals that control motor function. Deep brain stimulation relies on the precise placement of electrodes that carry small electrical currents to regions of the brain affected by Parkinson's disease. Finding just the right spot in the brain can make the difference between a successful outcome and worsening symptoms.

Seeing a 3-D image of the brain is the closest a doctor can get to working with the real thing. Flat images of a brain or any organ do not allow medical professionals to rotate the image or look at it from every possible angle to decide on the best treatment plan. "What we are trying to do in our virtual reality lab is come up with new ways to leverage technology to help doctors and nurses, or any medical professional, do what they do better. And how better than with 3D visualization," says Justin Sutherland, an assistant professor in the University of Ottawa's Department of Radiology. Sutherland helped design a VR imaging program that gives surgeons a remarkably comprehensive view of the brain of Parkinson's patients. "We think the technology has only reached that point now. We're now at a place where we want to pursue the avenue of clinicians-as-users."[21]

Rehabilitation and Recovery with VR

Doctors and other medical professionals are not the only ones benefiting from the boom in VR technology. Patients recovering from surgery, strokes, or other health challenges, for example, can utilize VR programs in their rehabilitation and physical therapy. Allen DeNiear suffered a stroke that left one of his hands with limited strength and flexibility. Traditional rehabilitation would simply have a stroke patient open and close the affected hand dozens of times. With the help of a VR flight simulator that requires the use of that hand to steer the plane on a computer screen, DeNiear made rapid strides in his recovery. "As you're playing the game, it breaks the monotony of what you're supposed to be doing," he says. "If I didn't have the games, it would be a lot slower. It helped speed the process up, I think."[22]

VR technology is also helping accident victims and others who need help relearning how to walk with better balance and confidence. VR programs can "trick" the brain by showing patients virtual legs and feet taking normal steps so that the users' brains will mimic the actions with their legs and feet. Paraplegic patients, such as those in Duke University's Walk Again Project, wear a robotic exoskeleton, a mechanical framework worn on the body, that responds to brain signals. With the combination of seeing their virtual legs moving and controlling the exoskeleton that actually moves

Midwives Train with Virtual Babies

A midwife is a person trained to assist an expectant mother with the delivery of her baby. Midwives typically receive classroom training and rely on textbooks and videos to better understand pregnancy and learn the skills necessary for a safe and healthy birth. But as with other aspects of health care, midwifery is getting the VR treatment too.

While wearing a digital headset, midwifery students at Australia's University of Newcastle can observe a baby growing inside a highly detailed, life-sized, 3-D figure of a woman. One of the most important lessons this VR program can provide is how to identify when a baby is in a potentially dangerous position prior to birth. Donovan Jones, a university lecturer and leader of the VR project, says:

> We can show them what happens when a baby is not in an ideal position for birth. At the moment we teach with dolls and pelvises, and I can tell you firsthand from being a student, as well as an educator, the position of the placenta is one of the hardest things to learn, and yet it's absolutely one of the most imperative things to know. If a midwife can't identify its position and lets the woman go into natural labor with the baby obstructed, the baby's life is at serious risk.

Jones says the virtual mother and child act as a bridge between the classroom and the delivery suite, where very real mothers and their babies will start their new lives together.

Quoted in Anita Beaumont. "Midwifery Students Use Virtual Reality to Learn the Stages of Pregnancy with 3D Female Figure," *Newcastle Herald* (Newcastle, Australia), March 1, 2018. www.newcastleherald.com.au.

their real legs, people who have not walked in years are able to take slow, steady steps and further enhance their recovery.

VR games are also being used to complement other types of physical therapy, though experts say it is unlikely that VR will ever eliminate the exercises and activities required in traditional rehabilitation processes. Simple skills such as lifting a box, throwing a ball, using eating utensils, or moving side to side often must be relearned in a physical therapy setting, but these can be taught with a little fun in a VR environment. "I think that these games can provide a very useful adjunct that can potentially offer some extra benefits," says Danielle Levac of Northeastern University's ReGame laboratory. "What we don't know enough of is when you learn a skill in a virtual environment, to what extent does that actually help you get better at that skill in real life?"[23]

Easing Real-World Anxiety

While transporting patients to a virtual environment can help improve injury rehabilitation and physical therapy, mental health therapy and emotional challenges can also benefit from the use of this new technology. VR's path to virtual environments is giving patients and their therapists new spaces to treat crippling phobias, post-traumatic stress disorder, and general anxiety. The technology can place individuals in simulated traumatic situations but do so in a controlled environment to help them overcome

The US Army is using VR to re-create wartime experiences, in hopes of helping veterans cope with post-traumatic stress disorder (PTSD).

those fears. VR environments that re-create wartime experiences, for example, allow military veterans to deal with the source of their PTSD in a safe, controlled way under the supervision of a therapist. "We tell the patients initially that this is going to be a very uncomfortable process," says Florida therapist Keith Smith. "So as a therapist, I'm going to be looking for signs of physical arousal—shaking, teary-eyed, muscle tension, those types of things."[24] He adds that veterans tend to become calmer with each VR session and as they share more about their experiences.

Similarly, a person with a serious fear of flying can sit in a simulated airplane cabin and wear a VR headset that re-creates takeoff, landing, and flying in a plane while a therapist provides helpful reassurance during the virtual plane ride. This sort of treatment is known as exposure therapy, and it can be effective for people with issues ranging from claustrophobia to social anxiety.

interactive
Allowing for a two-way exchange of information between a computer and its human user

Likewise, VR experiences that turn frightening or negative situations into pleasant ones can help patients become less stressed and more confident in their surroundings. "Most treatments, up until now, have done an OK job at reducing negative [symptoms of depression], but a very poor job at helping patients become more positive,"[25] says University of California, Los Angeles, researcher Michelle Craske, who is hoping to develop more interactive VR programs that help patients with depression learn to strike up positive conversations with characters in the VR experience.

Using VR to treat depression is still a relatively new concept. But environments that encourage social interaction—whether with fictional characters in a VR scenario or with other people meeting or playing in the VR environment—can help individuals whose depression limits their social interaction. Likewise, VR experiences that encourage physical activity, even if it is just walking or gentle game playing, address a common challenge of depression—a tendency to be sedentary. And one of the more interesting VR-based applications for depression therapy seeks to reduce self-criticism and boost self-compassion, which are two areas that typically need attention in depression sufferers. In a 2018 study in the United Kingdom, researchers placed adults with depression in a VR environment. Within this environment, the adult comforted a virtual crying child and the child responded to the empathy and kind words of the adult. In the next part of the study, the scene was reversed: the depressed adult was personified by a crying child, who heard and took comfort from the same words. In this way, the subjects learned they could tap into a sense of empathy for others and use some of those same feelings and words to comfort themselves. Improvements in self-compassion were noted, and the participants tended to be less critical of themselves after seeing themselves comfort someone else and be comforted by those same words. "Self-criticism is a huge vulnerability factor across a wide range of disorders," says Chris Brewing, the researcher who led the study. "So it's not inconceivable that if you can reduce that, this technique could be an effective standalone treatment for a proportion of people, where self-criticism is the main driving factor."[26]

Charting Health Outcomes

Aside from learning new behaviors or finding a healthier outlook, patients can experience something through VR that has previously been unattainable. They can see different models of themselves in the future: one that simulates a healthy lifestyle and one that reveals what might happen if they do not take their health seriously, such as serious weight gain or having sun-damaged or smoking-damaged skin.

Walter Greenleaf, a neuroscientist at Stanford University, developed a VR app that uses current images of a patient to create a personal avatar that can change dramatically according to various outcomes of healthy or unhealthy choices. Greenleaf says:

One of the big problems that we have as humans to change our behavior is we don't see the results right away; it might take months before we see the results of our decisions and our actions, but with a virtual environment we can see it right away. . . . Most of the work on this has been done with Stanford undergraduate students. Believe me, all it takes is age progressing their avatar by five years and they'll pay attention to their behavior. It's very scary.[27]

Training and Healing

The research into the effectiveness of VR in training medical students or helping patients in rehabilitation or mental health therapy is showing encouraging signs. Not all experiments with VR are showing groundbreaking results, but the consensus is that the use of VR is only going to grow in the health care field. And as the technology improves, the effectiveness of virtual reality in helping teach and heal will improve too.

CHAPTER THREE

Education

Videos and the internet helped propel the classroom from a textbook- and lecture-based environment to one in which technology is an indispensable part of teaching and learning. VR is set to take education to the next level by providing students immersive experiences that might have been unimaginable not that long ago.

That means field trips to the Great Wall of China and into a microscopic cell. It means interacting with fellow students thousands of miles away in a classroom that seems like a single shared space. It also means meeting the great figures from history, creating artwork in virtual space, designing games and robots, studying the surface of Mars, and countless other learning opportunities made possible by VR developers who want to give students learning experiences that no previous generation of learners has had.

VR can do what a paper-and-ink textbook cannot do: make any subject come alive to students who want or need more than words on the page or even words and pictures on a flat computer screen. "Every time that a new technology comes out, it quickly applies itself to some form of education," says Baptiste Grève, founder of the educational VR company Unimersiv. "VR will follow the same path. In fact, at some point in the future, people might not even have to go to schools—places of learning could be in VR spaces instead. As this happens, we want to be the place where you can go to learn absolutely anything."[28]

Virtual Field Trips

Virtual reality is all about transporting users to new, old, and imaginary places. It is not surprising then, that, virtual field trips to anywhere on or off Earth are at the heart of educational VR. A school field trip to the zoo to see an elephant up close can help children make a connection to these mighty animals. A new generation of VR experiences is allowing students to see elephants in their native habitat, roaming the savannas of Africa, drinking from watering holes alongside wildebeests, and interacting with other members of their herd.

A company called vEcotours provides students with VR experiences like an African tour. After presenting the experience one day at Jeffersonville, Vermont's Cambridge Elementary School, representatives from vEcotours challenged the students

A new generation of VR technology enables students to see elephants in their native habitat, roaming the savannas of Africa and interacting with other members of their herd.

to research what they had seen and come up with their own narration that could be added to the video in VR experiences other students could enjoy. Other VR field trips help students take the plunge to the Great Barrier Reef or take a tour of the International Space Station. "When you are able to put a person in a place, they will remember it,"[29] says Tom Furness, a VR pioneer and founding director of the Human Interface Technology Laboratory at the University of Washington.

The number of companies offering VR field trips is expanding. In addition to vEcotours, Nearpod, and Google Expeditions, other brands are meeting the growing demand from schools as well. Funding remains the biggest obstacle, even though the education sector is expected to spend about $6 billion in AR and VR technology in 2023. Much of that money is coming from grants awarded to individual schools and teachers. Fortunately, the price of VR headsets is dropping (around $200 each), which should allow more schools to "send" students across the country and across the universe.

Going Where Modern Students Cannot Otherwise Go

Virtual reality allows students to visit more than just other continents today. With technology limited only by imagination and inspiration, VR environments can welcome student visitors into places and events from centuries ago. One VR program takes users to Rome's Temple of Venus—not in its ruined form today, but when it was new, with towering columns and shining white marble welcoming Romans in the first century CE. "For me, time travel is something we can get pretty close to using VR," says Jason Kingsley, a cofounder of Rebellion and the founder of a history-themed YouTube channel. "I'm quite excited about the idea of exploring castles when they were first being built or going back to ancient Rome and just wandering through that landscape."[30]

Virtual field trips are also taking students to places that are only accessible with the magic of computer technology, like the human heart or a distant galaxy. "VR education can present

Want to Paint a Rain Forest?

The simulated worlds of VR can take students to places real and unreal. Through VR, students can spend the morning exploring the Amazon rain forest and, in the afternoon, sit in their classroom brainstorming solutions to save it. A week later, those same students can use a VR headset, a paintbrush-like controller, and a program called Tilt Brush from Google to virtually paint their own brightly colored jungles, bringing up close something that otherwise would be exotic and far away. Students envision a rain forest and its abundant and varied wildlife and then paint it in three dimensions. The students choose how plants, animals, and even the sunlight look, making artwork in a virtual space.

The rain forest project, led by Greenwich, Connecticut art teacher Cheryl Iozzo at North Street School, allowed her to exchange student art from the United States with students in Guatemala and then take her students on a VR excursion to the artwork depicted in the Guatemalan students' pictures. Like other forms of hands-on learning that reinforce information and make it more meaningful to students, VR-enabled art and research is simply the next step in the marriage of technology and education, Iozzo says. "There hasn't been a new art medium invented in a long time," she says. "Tech is not going away, so how are we going to use it?"

Quoted in Jo Kroeker, "Students Create, Explore New Worlds Through Virtual Reality," AP News, June 19, 2019. https://apnews.com.

course material like no textbook or video ever could," says Matt "Stompz" Carrell, cohost of the *Pod VR* podcast. "You can shrink students down to the cellular level or grow them to the size of the universe. With VR you can give children their own 'Magic School Bus' education."[31] At Mercy Career & Technical High School in Philadelphia, students in the science and health occupation program use *The Body VR: Journey Inside a Cell*, a VR experience that gives them a molecular-level view of a cell's nucleus and membrane. "I felt like I could touch everything,"[32] says Mercy student Isaac Davids. Biology teacher Kathleen Logan explains that VR can bring textbook lessons to life. "Biology is a lot of material and vocabulary," she says. "VR really helps to make a connection with what we're talking about. It's putting all the parts in context."[33]

Virtual field trips have another advantage: cost. Many schools must hold fund-raisers just to send students to a theatrical production in their hometown, and colleges tend to put the responsibility of paying for study abroad on the students, rather than finance that kind of experiential learning themselves. VR changes all of that. "Out of classroom experiences can have a profound impact on students but they are often expensive and difficult to organize," Unimersiv's Grève says. "VR can help solve this by providing users—including, potentially, school children—with simulated experiences that involve less travel, less paperwork and less organization. VR is the future of education."[34]

Aside from the investment in VR headsets and related technology, VR environments require no travel costs. "VR could change how educational institutions think about budgeting, as well," says Lyron Bentovim, a professor and chief executive of the VR/AR company the Glimpse Group. "Let's say you wanted to simulate what it's like to work as a geologist or teach a class about manufacturing in Japan. Now you can take the whole class to Japan with the click of a button."[35]

Lessons for Everyone

Some VR experiences do not need to take students or adults far away to be eye-opening lessons. A VR simulation developed by Juliano Calil, a professor at the Middlebury Institute of International Studies in California and a researcher into coastal adaptation, brings one of the greatest dangers of climate change into the communities that might be most affected by it. He and partners from various local governments and universities are creating VR simulations for coastal communities facing the threat of sea-level rise as polar ice caps melt.

Simulating the future of cities such as Long Beach, California, and Baltimore, Maryland, Calil and his partners show how rising seas will eventually flood various neighborhoods. In a presentation in Baltimore, residents slipped on VR headsets and watched in shock as their homes and the parks and shops they frequent would be slowly overtaken by water if rising waters continue unabated. The users have a controller that brings the floodwaters up as a narrator explains what is happening and why. Pastor Eric Johnson of Baltimore's Union Baptist Church, who attended the presentation, comments, "You hear about global warming and the effects of it, but to really be able to see it in real time is an eye-opener. It shows you this is something we needed to work on, like yesterday."[36]

Improving Communication Skills

Whether it is teaching students Japanese, Spanish, or Latin, studying vocabulary words seldom gets students excited and anxious to do more. But a VR app called CoSpaces allows students to, among many things, create vocabulary flash cards in a VR environment. Wearing VR goggles, students in an Oregon classroom shared their creations with each other, turning a lesson in Spanish vocabulary into a fun activity that could be

VR technology helps turn learning a foreign language into a fun, interactive experience.

adjusted and reexperienced by students without the students getting bored. The school's instructional technology teacher, Benjamin Lloyd, says:

> What we noticed right away: the students created some-thing that they could come back to. That was the exciting part to me. It wasn't some set of flashcards they made and then it got stuck somewhere and they never looked at it again. The whole class was creating and they could share their projects with each other. This gave way to lots of opportunities to experience the same vocabulary in slightly different ways—without any more work on the part of the teacher.[37]

Applying that newly acquired vocabulary is yet another way VR is changing education. Rather than have high school Spanish students practice dialogues with each other in the classroom, teachers using VR programs like Unimersiv or Busuu can get students in their classroom in the United States to interact virtually with Spanish-speaking students in other nations who are anxious to practice their English with students in the United States. With VR language apps, students can pick up an item they are identifying in a new language or get help with pronunciation from other kids who are native speakers. "The best way to learn a language still remains going to that country and being fully immersed. We want to provide the second best way," says Antoine Sakho, head of product development at Busuu. "VR won't make you fluent, but it can add a nice immersive, story-driven touch to language learning to make it more fun and give you some basic knowledge."[38]

Public speaking, another dreaded activity in school, is also getting the VR treatment with experiences that allow students to practice getting up in front of virtual audiences of varying sizes and in varying environments. Speaking to an audience that will not laugh or make faces can ease the anxiety for kids who are uncomfortable giving speeches or reading in public. But even more than that, some VR environments, such as one developed at Lehman College's Center for Student Leadership Development, in New York City, can monitor whether the speaker is making good eye contact with the audience, track how fast or slow the person is speaking, and actually offer suggestions for improvement. Students can practice in virtual settings such as a brightly lit classroom, an intimidating corporate boardroom, and others. There is even an interview mode that poses questions to the speaker—typical interview questions provided by companies such as Google, Apple, and Procter & Gamble. "It felt great speaking to a virtual audience," says John Carlos Rodriguez, a graduate student at Lehman College. "I felt like it gave me great practice. Presentations are such a big portion of graduate school, so this came in handy."[39]

Not all students are as comfortable speaking in front of peers as this student. But now students can use VR technology to practice speaking in front of a virtual audience, which can reduce anxiety about making speeches in public.

Getting Graduates Ready for the Real World

The *real world* is a term often used by high school and college students to refer to life after graduation. The real world means having a job. And to help their students prepare for the real world, college professors are turning to some virtual worlds. Learning how to be successful in the business world means mastering skills like negotiating, making presentations, and networking with strangers. These are all people skills that cannot be taught as easily as accounting or marketing can from textbooks and lectures. Therefore, to help its students learn some of those necessary, so-called soft skills, Fordham University is placing students in VR business environments through its Exploring Entrepreneurship class.

Several students don headsets and interact with each other and virtual characters, while the professor and other students observe the action on a large screen in the classroom so they can offer feedback later. Students, for example, must lead high-stakes negotiations in a conference room or get to know strangers in a corporate setting. "Your brain actually assumes you've experienced the simulated environment, and it brings educational concepts to life for students," says Bentovim, whose Glimpse Group developed the business school VR program. "When they leave class, they don't say, 'We learned about negotiating today'; they say, 'I negotiated today,' or, 'I led a business meeting today.' When you have the headset on, it feels real, and that experience creates confidence."[40]

improvising
Creating or performing something without any preparation

Similar VR simulations are also in place at other business schools such as the Massachusetts Institute of Technology (MIT) and Stanford University. One of MIT's programs allows students to become United Nations delegates negotiating agreements on climate change, reinforcing the importance of improvising, negotiating, and public speaking on subjects that have important and long-lasting impacts. And some colleges are using VR to teach team-building skills, like simulations in which a group of students have to dismantle a bomb or encourage each other to overcome their fears and walk across a virtual tightrope between the tops of two Tokyo skyscrapers high above the city.

dismantle
Disconnect the parts or pieces of an object

Student Athletes Dodge Virtual Tacklers

There is an old saying that 90 percent of sports success is mental, not physical. While that percentage may be debatable, VR simulations used by Stanford University football players demonstrate that there is certainly a lot going on in the brain affecting athletic performance. Stanford coach David Shaw was an early proponent of having his student athletes try VR simulations to help reinforce skills they were learning on the practice field. Quarterbacks and defensive linemen put on their headsets and were suddenly in game-like conditions, with other virtual players coming at them and the game clock ticking. "This crazy thing happens when guys get in the VR—usually within 10 minutes, most of them start to sweat," Shaw says, noting that the real players were barely moving. "But their brain is seeing these visuals, these different formations and motions and plays and defenses. The more they see them, the quicker they react."

VR technology is being used in many sports, and at all levels. Some Olympic skiers, for instance, use headsets and stand on specially designed platforms that can simulate the twists and turns of a downhill race. Sports success may not be precisely 90 percent mental, but VR illustrates that much of it can be credited to what is learned in the brain, not just in the rest of the body.

Quoted in Yuki Noguchi, "Virtual Reality Goes to Work, Helping Train Employees," *Morning Edition*, NPR, October 8, 2019. www.npr.org.

Training for VR Careers

Bomb dismantling and mile-high tightrope stunts may not qualify as real-world scenarios for most people, but just about everybody who has worked for a living knows it can often be a challenge to find a good job and to have job skills that are in demand. Given the rising use and demand for VR software and hardware, people who want to make the virtual world their real-world career are finding opportunities in unexpected places.

scenario
A sequence of events, especially when imagined

In eastern Kentucky, for example, where the coal industry and related businesses kept unemployment rates low for a long time, the need for alternative job opportunities has been growing for many years. To help displaced coal miners learn new job skills and to help high school students learn skills that will help keep them closer to home, Berea College invested in dozens of VR consoles to spur the training and possible future employment of VR specialists. High school students learn about VR technology during the day, and unemployed coal miners work with the equipment in the evening. "We're making sure that the young people in this community have the skill set that they need to not only benefit from the emergence of this new technology, but to drive it," says Adam Edelen, vice chair of Lobaki, a VR firm based in Mississippi. "We're creating new economic opportunities in a community that's dealing with economic difficulty."[41]

As an educational tool, VR can immerse students in rain forests, far-off galaxies, and places that exist only in the imagination. It can bring people from the other side of the world into the classroom, too. The limits of VR in education lie only in the technology of the moment and the ability of schools and teachers to purchase the equipment necessary to make these experiences possible for their students. But as costs start to come down and VR becomes not just an expensive toy but an integral part of a twenty-first-century education, people can expect to see and hear about more virtual field trips and memorable lessons learned via headset and goggles.

CHAPTER FOUR

In the Workplace

Virtual reality may be mostly associated with escapist entertainment like video games or with experiences that place users in far-flung and exotic destinations. But one of VR's most rapidly growing uses is in department stores, factories, offices, oil rigs, and just about anywhere people work for a living. Rather than using VR as a temporary escape from reality into a virtual fantasy world, businesses and government agencies are using job-focused VR experiences to train new employees, bring coworkers together in virtual environments, introduce new products to customers, and even screen job candidates.

While there is no way to tell how much the workplace will be altered by VR, it is clear that big companies and the government take it seriously. Having seen how the personal computer (PC), internet, and smartphones changed business across all industries, companies are not dismissing VR as a fad or a toy. A report by the international investment bank Goldman Sachs suggests that VR could be "as game-changing as the advent of the PC."[42]

High-Tech Training

While the military is using VR systems to train jet pilots and pro sports teams are using them to boost player performance, most VR workplace training environments are not especially glamorous or adventurous. Still, VR technology is helping workers learn how to do their jobs better. Walmart, for example, has had more than 1 million employees use VR programs to improve their interactions with customers, especially in situations like the Black Friday frenzy of shoppers that cannot exactly be duplicated in a role-playing scenario with a few workers and a trainer in a conference room. The Black Friday program places workers in a crowded store, where they must respond to a wide range of questions and demands from shoppers. The employees can pause the program to ask questions, and their supervisors can identify issues that may need additional training or explanation. "The biggest advantage for us at Walmart is our associates," says Brock McKeel, Walmart's senior director of digital operations. "Anything we can do to make our associates better, and help them take care of their customers, is an advantage for us."[43]

VR works well as a training tool because the brain processes a VR experience—the characters, settings, and scenarios—as though it were a real experience. Reacting in a realistic virtual environment, employees are more likely to respond in the real world in ways that worked in their virtual episodes. "People learn

Shoppers wait in a checkout line at a Walmart on Black Friday. Walmart is using VR technology to train its employees to deal with the issues that can arise during extremely busy shopping days.

by doing . . . getting feedback on mistakes, and then repeating and iterating,"[44] says Jeremy Bailenson, founder of Stanford University's Virtual Human Interaction Lab.

Verizon trained employees with VR simulations to prepare them for in-store robberies, an unfortunate but all-too-common concern in places where smartphones are sold. The simulated holdups stir some upsetting emotions, but the goal is to make sure employees can get through such an experience calmly and safely. "By the end of the experience they feel like they've been robbed three times, and by the third time their confidence is significantly higher,"[45] says Lou Tedrick, who heads up Verizon's learning and development. The Verizon robbery simulation has another benefit—assisting law enforcement by teaching participants how to pick up important details about a suspect, says Michael Mason, chief of security for Verizon. "If nothing else, then an employee understands what he or she should be looking at in the bad guy . . . and if that helps identify a bad guy and take him off the street, then that means they can't repeat that activity."[46]

Risk-Free Training for Dangerous Jobs

Employees can also acquire lessons about handling dangers of other sorts through VR simulations. VR environments have a very important luxury that real-world, hands-on training cannot provide: safety. When handling big, dangerous, and expensive machines, workers need to be sure about what they are doing. Training someone who might cause a serious and costly accident is a big risk for an employer. But sitting that person down with a VR headset and giving him or her countless chances to learn in a simulated setting is making a lot of sense to companies around the world.

The oil and gas industry, for example, is overcoming the dangers of drilling and the challenges of finding petroleum with the help of VR. Oil companies are using VR to train people on oil rig work so they can master skills without the dangers and expense of putting them on actual rigs in remote parts of the world.

Oil companies are using VR to train workers to do difficult or dangerous jobs before sending them to actual oil rigs in remote parts of the world.

At ExxonMobil, new employees use AR technology when learning about all the systems at work in a refinery or processing plant, watching dials virtually turn and sensors indicate problems when no real crisis is occurring. Mats W. Johansson, CEO of EON Reality, says:

> The Immersive 3D Operator Training Simulator will change how operators and plant crews train on existing facilities and even before a facility is operational. Working with ExxonMobil, we have created an immersive training tool to ensure that entire plant operation teams have practiced actual procedures together on a virtual facsimile of their plant. This is truly a flight simulator for plant operations.[47]

Construction workers can also enter VR environments to learn how to spot flaws in construction or learn to operate heavy machinery without the risks and expenses involved with real hands-on training. At some point in anyone's training, actual on-the-job learning must occur, but industries are cutting costs and risks by first sending their new hires through a risk-free environment in which mistakes never cause damage.

Saving Time and Money

The efficient use of heavy machinery and high-tech equipment is improved with VR and AR applications, too. Rolls-Royce and Qatar Airways use VR to train their engineers. Rolls-Royce's massive engines that power Qatar Airway's Airbus A350s must be separated in order to be transported and then must be reassembled. Engineers, who must also be able to maintain and repair the engines, are practicing these skills on virtual engines. This saves both companies time and money, since engines used to have to be physically transported to training facilities at great expense and with some risk that damage could occur in the process. "At Rolls-Royce, we are designing, testing, and maintaining engines in the digital realm, so it makes sense that we bring cutting-edge technology to our training programs," says Chris Cholerton, president of Rolls-Royce Civil Aerospace. "In the same way pilots complete elements of their training in a simulator, certain engineering tasks can be taught through virtual reality."[48]

Steve Buckland, a customer and product training manager at Rolls-Royce and the developer of the VR training program, has plans to expand VR and AR uses, though he insists that hands-on experience with actual engines and equipment will always be a component of engineer education. Buckland says:

Virtual reality has a valuable application here. It's going to save time, money, and frees up engines that could otherwise be on aircraft, keeping passengers moving. The future is exciting. We're looking at creating holograms of an engine that we can use to teach in a classroom, or augmented reality that can be overlaid over a real engine to show technical information. Nothing will beat learning with an engine, and this will never be replaced, but new technology is allowing us to be innovative with the ways we teach engineers.[49]

But even if the equipment is not very expensive, there are still financial incentives to using VR in training. Walmart claims its VR training for store managers cuts training time and costs for Black Friday shopping madness. And the truck and trailer rental giant United Rentals reports shaving 40 percent off its employee training time with VR experiences. Small businesses are even getting in on the act with VR and AR training, in part because an estimated 40 percent of employees who complain of poor training quit their jobs within the first year.

Better Information Retention Through VR Training

Restaurants face high employee turnover for a lot of reasons, including lower-than-average pay and challenging working conditions like late nights and long shifts. So, with restaurant owners having to train new employees frequently, anything that can reduce that training time and get new hires up to speed quickly will help. One study found that VR can cut training times for many restaurants in half. Restaurants do not always have the necessary number of people available for training and shadowing, but a new hire can slip on a VR headset and learn the job by interacting with virtual coworkers and virtual, yet hungry, customers. The national restaurant chain Honeygrow has a VR training program. "We feel people will retain information much better if they're able to engage and interact in a meaningful way," says Honeygrow's Jen Denis. "This generation has grown up with video, gaming, and technology. More and more, we learn by doing rather than reading."[50]

Taking Flight Without Leaving the Ground

Flight simulators have been used in pilot training since before World War I, and they have helped commercial pilots learn to handle 747s and navy pilots to become familiar with what they will encounter trying to land on an aircraft carrier. (They are also among the more popular home VR simulations for non-pilots.) The US Air Force and US Navy are providing more training on $1,000 VR systems instead of in jets costing millions of dollars. At Sheppard Air Force Base in Texas, VR flight simulators are used to train new pilots from around the world. The simulations are so realistic that one instructor says he often sees future pilots' "knees quiver" during some of the virtual maneuvers. "The [VR practice] essentially gives them the ability to visualize some of the things that they'll experience airborne so that once they do get airborne, they're able to take those reference pictures that they saw in mixed reality and apply them to their training in the air, hopefully making their air time training more valuable," says Lieutenant Colonel Jason Turner, director of Strategic Initiatives at Sheppard. For civilians who want to get in on the action, the Smithsonian Institution's National Air and Space Museum offers visitors VR flight simulators for some of the nation's most famous military aircraft, including the P-51 Mustang, F/A-18 Hornet, and the F-16 Fighting Falcon. And 360-degree barrel rolls are free for those with a strong stomach and a taste for adventure.

Quoted in John Ingle, "Pilot Training Moving at the Speed of Innovation," Hill Air Force Base, February 7, 2019. www.hill.af.mil.

Other studies show that VR training also helps new employees retain more of what they learn in training. One study found that about half of what new employees learn in orientation and training is forgotten in six weeks. But because VR involves workers by having them go through meetings, customer encounters, and other parts of their job rather than just listen to managers talk about those things, the new employees tend to hold on to that new information longer. Walmart's research found that employees retain about 10 to 15 percent more information through

VR training than they did the old-fashioned way, with classroom exercises, videos, and online study. And workers trained with AR tools tend to be better able to transmit their new skills and information to their peers.

VR continues to prove a convenient tool for business in many fields. Insurance companies, for example, need their employees to have skills such as sizing up damage to a home. Farmers Insurance used to send new agents to a special company house that was "damaged" to teach them how to evaluate what is and is not covered by homeowners insurance. But it was always the same house with the same damage. Recognizing the boundless opportunities of VR, Farmers Insurance invested in a VR simulation that can train new employees on more than five hundred types of damage. Eventually, Farmers and other insurance companies want to provide customers VR simulations that will help them learn how to avoid accidents to cut down on the number of claims. And instead of sending a team of representatives to handle various parts of a homeowner's claim, insurance compa-

Insurance companies have begun using VR to train employees to assess property damage from storms and other natural disasters.

nies are looking to develop the technology whereby one person wearing a 360-degree camera could walk through a home and reveal all the damage to others at the company.

Hiring with a Headset

Even before a new employee is hired, companies try to make sure the people they bring on board are a good fit for the job. The National Football League, for example, offers a VR app to general managers to train them in interviewing college players they may want to draft. Often there is an initial interview between a job applicant and someone in human resources (a company's department responsible for hiring). Walmart, which employs more than 2 million people around the world, has started using VR in screening job candidates with programs that ask them a series of questions. How the job candidates answer can often determine whether they get a second interview and possibly a job offer, says Andy Trainor, Walmart's head of learning. "With all the data you get from VR, you can see where they look. You can see how they move and how they react," Trainor says. "You could do an interview in VR and based on the way they answer the questions, you can preselect whether or not they'd be a good fit for that role."[51]

VR may also help potential employees decide whether the employer would be a good fit for the employee as well. Alexandra Berger, senior vice president of marketing and communications for the British electronics firm RS Components, envisions a time when VR will make the interviewing process easier for candidates who live far from a company's headquarters. "VR can also provide candidates with the option to take a virtual tour of the office to gain an understanding of where they could be working without having to travel in,"[52] she says.

Commerce and Collaboration

Crossing the miles with technology is commonplace in business today. Videoconferences bring together work colleagues spread

More VR Means More VR Jobs . . . Eventually

As VR's presence grows in the workplace and society in general, the number of jobs in VR and AR will likely grow too. Certainly, tech experts experienced in user interface and user experience will be needed. But people with an interest in VR but who have training and experience in marketing, business development, education, and other industries will also find plenty of opportunities in the future world of VR. Steve Santamaria, chief operating officer of Envelop VR in Seattle, Washington, says that visionaries, project managers, and other nonengineering professionals will shape the way VR fits into and changes society. "But today, early on, pre-customers, it will be the technical people visioning and creating the VR products," he says. "Later, after the industry is established you will see more of the mature industry jobs being listed."

And that growth has been steadily expanding in recent years. VRFocus, an online industry publication, reported that from 2014 to 2019, the share of job postings per million on the online job board Indeed increased by 1,314.44 percent, while VR job searches increased by 951.89 percent in the same time frame. And unlike so many tech jobs that are located in California, the place to launch VR and AR careers may be North Carolina. The cities of Charlotte and Raleigh, home of Epic Games, are among the top metropolitan areas of the country for AR and VR jobs.

Quoted in Caroline Zaayer Kaufman, "How to Land a Job in Virtual Reality Tech," Monster, 2020. www.monster.com.

across the map, and online shopping for everything from groceries to automobiles is available to all consumers. While online computer technology has allowed people to do business in virtual spaces, VR may be bringing customers and companies together, and employees from branch offices together, in ways that may have seemed like science fiction not long ago. "The concept here is that VR should feel less like switching between apps, and more like exploring new worlds in a VR native environment," says Dan O'Brien, HTC Vive's general manager for the Americas. HTC Vive is a VR headset and platform that is used in business, gaming, and many other fields. "We believe the next jumping point will be in VR collaboration, so that people can more easily meet and work in VR,"[53] says O'Brien.

And as a shopping device, VR headsets are being used to introduce brand-new automobiles to potential buyers who want to not just look at a car, but know what it might be like to slip in behind the wheel. VR simulations allow shoppers to take detailed tours of all kinds of stores from the comfort of their homes. And augmented programs can project real-life items such as furniture to show what a new couch might look like in a home. "The implementation of AR and VR in retail offers new methods the industry can operate on," says Naveen Joshi, CEO of the tech company Allerin. "Both these technologies are extending and expanding on traditional services offered by the retail industry. The future of retail deeply involves technology and AR and VR are going to play a huge role in this services industry."[54]

collaboration
Working with others to create or produce something

CHAPTER FIVE

Travel

A high school student is interested in a college a thousand miles away. A history buff longs to tour a museum in a country that is an ocean away. An older adult with health challenges that make flying or traveling long distances by car difficult has always wanted to visit Paris. Currently, all these individuals can go online and see pictures or videos of those places of interest. But with the assistance of VR, the student can walk across that distant college campus, taking in the sights and sounds of what could be the next step in their education. And that history enthusiast could put on a VR headset and get a close-up, if virtual, view of a foreign museum's artifacts from ancient times. And the person who always wanted to stroll by Parisian street cafés with the Eiffel Tower looming closer with every step can do just that—virtually anyway.

Stepping into virtual destinations of choice is getting easier all the time as VR technology improves and developers recognize a growing and varied market for travel-related simulations. Now anyone with access to a VR headset also has access to innumerable college campuses, museums, parks, and destinations, both natural and human-made, across the globe.

College Visits

Touring a college campus is a rite of passage for many high school students, but it is not always practical to physically visit all the colleges that interest them. Around the world, tech companies are teaming up with universities to provide virtual tours that do much more than walk students across campus and point out dorms and administration buildings.

GEAR UP NC, for example, crafted 360-degree tours of all sixteen schools in the University of North Carolina system and included stops at band practices, classrooms, labs, and intramural fields. GEAR UP is accompanied by a smartphone app and a chatbot to answer questions about various majors and admissions requirements. The project was headed up by Alexis Barnes, a graduate of the University of North Carolina. "I hope more people are able to see themselves in college and find a school that actually fits them,"[55] she says.

chatbot
A computer program designed to simulate human conversation

To see just how good a fit it might be, students need to get as close as they can to the buildings and places on campus, says Steve Johnson, founder of SeeBoundless, which produces VR and AR experiences of all kinds. Johnson adds, "Our goal with building virtual experiences was to get the students inside the buildings. We want to enhance the college tour experience and allow thousands of prospective students to virtually meet advisors, practice with the marching bands and feel what it's like to be in college, not just on a college campus."[56] Some schools use VR to help persuade interested students even after they have been accepted. The University of Oregon has sent cardboard VR goggles to accepted students in hopes that a VR experience will tip the scales in the school's favor and convince undecided students to make the university a top choice.

The growth of VR college tours comes at an ideal time, since high school students are applying to more colleges than in years past, according to a report by the National Association for College Admission Counseling. "Students are viewing the most sophisticated marketing outreach the world has ever known, and they're not going to be satisfied with old-fashioned postcards and fliers,"[57] says Stephanie Harff, assistant vice president of marketing

Technology companies and universities are teaming up to use VR to offer potential students virtual tours of college campuses.

and recruitment at the University of South Florida, which offers several virtual tour options. And for students who live especially far away, a virtual visit may be all they can get before making a decision. "International students are very unlikely to visit campus before showing up on day one," says Joe Lackner, director of web communications at Hanover College in Indiana. "The more we can show them of our campus, the better."[58]

Vacation Planning

Deciding where to go to college can be a life-altering choice. And even though vacation plans may not have the same kind of long-term impact, they nevertheless demand some careful consideration, especially given the costs of travel. While websites of resorts and other travel spots can entice travelers with gorgeous videos, photos, and descriptions of their amenities, nothing short of setting foot on the properties can match VR for letting users really get a sense of a possible vacation destination.

A purpose of travel-related VR tours is to offer virtual experiences to whet the appetites of potential visitors. A virtual vacation preview can also help customers decide exactly what they want to see and do. And rather than take the place of a real visit, a VR experience can make people more excited about seeing and doing the real thing.

The advantages of VR hotel and resort tours are plentiful. For example, one person in the family may want to take a closer look at the rooms and restaurants, while another may want to check out the beach or golf course. With comprehensive VR tours, everyone's interests can be satisfied, and each resort can offer its own personality with the tours it provides. For example, Le Franschhoek Hotel & Spa in South Africa starts its VR tour with a personal greeting by the manager, which is followed by a walk-through of the property offering 360-degree views throughout. "I think VR is definitely going to influence travelers on where they are going to spend their money," says travel writer John DiScala. "Nothing is ever going to compete with the real thing. You take a tour of these places, the rooms, the pool, the spa, it will really help with the spending decision but I don't think people are going to sit on the couch taking a wholly virtual vacation without wanting to actually go there."[59]

But it is not just the destinations that are luring potential visitors with 360-degree calling cards. The modes of travel themselves are showing off in VR. Cathay Pacific, a leading airline in travel to Asia, teamed with VR developer OmniVirt to create 360-degree VR ads to present potential travelers with the experience of being pampered on their luxurious transpacific flights. Carnival Cruise Line and other cruise ship companies are seeking to get new passengers to step aboard with immersive VR experiences that take users throughout the massive ships and introduce them to the entertainment they offer. Royal Caribbean Cruises, for instance, offers a VR aerial excursion as a way of introducing people to the company's trips and activities. "There are a lot of first-time cruisers who don't know what our excursions are about, so VR is a great way to give them a taste of what it's like to be 500 feet above the ground with the wind at your face in a hot air balloon,"[60] says Jay Schneider, of Royal Caribbean.

Diminishing Disability Limitations

Virtual experiences delivered through a VR headset can allow people with disabilities to enjoy activities that they might not be able to otherwise take part in. This experience can sometimes make it feel as though one's physical limitations have disappeared. "For those who are physically disabled, virtual reality means the potential to try out-of-reach experiences such as climbing a mountain, skateboarding or swimming in the sea, perhaps for the first time,"[61] says Claudia Cahalane, a writer who covers issues of concern to people with disabilities.

The escape factor provided by VR can provide therapeutic value for people coping with physical discomfort or emotional struggles brought on by loneliness or social isolation. Dr. Sonya Kim, a former emergency room physician who went on to start a VR company called One Caring Team, created a Hawaiian VR environment with those people in mind. Among her first clients were residents of an assisted living facility in California. Enjoying her Aloha VR program, which features a gorgeous sunset on a tropical beach, "allows them to forget their chronic pain, anxiety, the fact that they are alone," she says, adding that VR can be "a new care modality to bring to a senior care setting like this, to inspire them to live another day, where they're happy."[62]

therapeutic
Related to healing a disease or other health condition

Likewise, older adults who may be limited physically or financially from taking long trips can visit destinations around the globe, seeing people and places that would otherwise have been

Making It to Mars

Though human travelers may one day explore the edges of the solar system and the deep recesses of the Milky Way, the National Aeronautics and Space Administration's (NASA) farthest destination for a planned, manned mission is the red planet of Mars. But a virtual map of the galaxy allows scientists, engineers and wannabe explorers to blast off into the heart of the Milky Way without leaving Earth's gravity for a moment. The Exoplanet Excursions VR app takes visitors on a guided tour of the TRAPPIST-1 planetary system, the only known exoplanet (outside the solar system) system to include seven planets roughly the size of Earth.

And for that planned mission to Mars, VR has already helped pave the way for a successful outcome. NASA took satellite and telescopic images of Mars to create a VR environment that helped engineers and scientists prepare for the mission that placed the rover *Curiosity* on the Martian landscape in 2012. "Feeling like you're standing on Mars really gives you a different sense of Mars than just looking at the pictures," says Parker Abercrombie, leader of OnSight, a NASA project that used images supplied by *Curiosity* to create a virtual environment being studied by NASA scientists and astronauts.

Quoted in Astrobiology Magazine, "Mars Virtual Reality Award Wins NASA Award," October 13, 2018. www.astrobio.net.

impossible. "From reducing loneliness to transporting the infirm to far-flung places, without the need to travel, VR is enhancing the lives of senior citizens across the globe,"[63] says Sol Rogers, the founder and CEO of REWIND, a company that produces a wide range of VR and AR experiences.

Nursing homes and senior centers are buying VR headsets to give older adults experience that they thought might have passed them by. One popular app for seniors allows them to travel back in time for a bit. MyndVR puts users in a 1950s dance hall with actors in period clothing and a band playing the music of Frank Sinatra. The mental and emotional comfort that comes from seeing and

VR technology can allow people to travel back in time—for example, to experience the excitement of a 1950s dance with a live band. This technology can benefit older adults who have memory loss.

hearing familiar things can bring peace of mind to older adults and spark memories that may be fading. Another product, VR Genie, takes older adults all around the world to help them, at least virtually, tick things off their "bucket lists." A woman in Miami who left Cuba when she was very young took a VR trip back to her native country with VR Genie, an experience that she said after years in exile "gave life to her soul."[64]

Vacation on the Couch

Of course, VR vacations can be enjoyed by anyone, not just those who are kept close to home for physical or financial reasons. It is possible to take a virtual climb of Mount Everest with the Everest VR produced by Sólfar Studios. The experience is told in five chapters, starting with base camp and ending at the top of the legendary mountain, with a panoramic view of the Himalayas that can make some virtual climbers a little uneasy. "When we tried it out for the first time, we felt our knees go weak several times,"[65] says travel writer Tobey Grumet Segal.

One of the first and among the most popular VR travel experiences is presented by Google Earth. It uses satellite, aerial, and the 3-D-mapped Street View mode, so users can walk or fly around their virtual destinations. There is even a way to turn day into night with just a spin of the sun. Other VR travel apps take visitors along the azure waters surrounding Tahiti and through the Grand Canyon on a motorized kayak that gives users the chance to control the speed.

And for people willing to drive across town, digital spas are popping up around the world, giving customers unique virtual

Homemade VR Experiences

Affording the technology to produce breathtaking VR experiences in video games or theme parks, let alone the technical know-how, is still out of the reach of most consumers. But there are 360-degree cameras that people can take on vacation to make their own VR videos. Products such as GoPro Fusion (which is waterproof, making it ideal for capturing that snorkeling trip) and Insta360 (featuring a slow-motion feature) are roughly spherical in shape, with six or more cameras aimed in different directions to provide images surrounding the user wherever the cameras are taken. The cameras can be mounted on poles or handles or carried by hand. They can also take still pictures and normal videos that can be viewed on a smartphone or other device or uploaded to YouTube. But for people who want to relive their hike up Mount Hood in Oregon, their trek through a Costa Rican jungle, or just their walk up and down the hills of San Francisco, a 360-degree camera can create videos that can be downloaded to a VR headset and enjoyed countless times or be shared with others who could not be along for the fun. Costs for these cameras range from a few hundred to several thousand dollars.

vacations in specially designed relaxation rooms, with breezes timed to the images on screen, scents to match, and all enjoyed in the comfort of a massage chair. "I could see the wind flowing through the trees and then I could feel the breeze going across my body,"[66] says Lauren Felton, a customer of the digital spa Esqapes in Los Angeles.

Green Travel

Virtual brushes with nature may do much more than provide some temporary relaxation. They can allow VR travelers to see natural areas such as rain forests, coral reefs, polar ice caps, or

With the help of VR, people can experience visits to remote locations, such as the Great Barrier Reef. Activists hope that such experiences can help build awareness of the urgent need to preserve fragile ecosystems.

other regions in crisis so they can learn more about what must be done to improve the environment and save the planet. "Virtual reality can give everyone, regardless of where they live, the kind of experience needed to generate the urgency required to prevent environmental calamity,"[67] says Jeremy Bailenson, professor of communication at Stanford University. For example, the Google Expeditions project, designed to provide VR experiences to students, is viewed as a means of reaching students for whom classroom lectures and textbooks are not effective.

acidification
To make something like the ocean acidic, which makes it harder for certain plants and animals to survive

Immersive experiences with VR can help people see not just how things are today but how they might be if pollution, climate change, and other environmental problems continue unabated. Likewise, VR can also surround users with hopeful environments that could develop if people and governments take action. "The virtual reality platform allows someone who has never even been in the ocean to experience what ocean acidification can do to marine life," says Kristy Kroeker, assistant professor of ecology and environmental biology at the University of California, Santa Cruz, and a consultant on a VR project designed to educate the public in new ways. "We are visual creatures, and visual examples can be very striking."[68]

Dawn of a New Age

Traveling virtually to relaxing getaways in distant lands or times long ago or even worlds that never existed in real life is at the heart of VR. And it is that immersive experience and the feelings it conjures in everyone who journeys into VR that mark the next big change in how people interact with technology. From the early days of the computer, and certainly for as long as the internet has been around, engineers and scientists have developed ways to consume, share, and store unlimited amounts of information. It is termed the "information age" because computers allow people to gather so much information and use it countless ways.

But as more people step into virtual environments, society as a whole is stepping into the next era of computer-driven change. Kent Bye, host of the *Voices of VR Podcast*, says:

> Right now our culture is just at the very beginning of shift from the Information Age to the Experiential Age where our attention will be primarily focused on experiencing visceral emotions rather than consuming vast data streams of information. . . . Virtual reality, augmented reality, and mixed reality experiences will be helping to drive this new Renaissance where technology more accurately reflects and amplifies the full breadth and complexity of the human experience.[66]

SOURCE NOTES

Introduction: Virtual Reality Opens Doors to Real and Unreal Worlds

1. Quoted in *Arkenea* (blog), "16 Experts Predict the Future of Virtual Reality," 2016. https://arkenea.com.
2. Quoted in Rachel Arthur, "Amazon Introduces VR Kiosks for Prime Day," Current Daily, July 16, 2018. https://thecurrent daily.com.
3. Quoted in *Arkenea* (blog), "16 Experts Predict the Future of Virtual Reality."

Chapter One: Entertainment

4. Peter Rubin, "Want to Know the Real Future of AR/VR? Ask Their Devs," *Wired*, August 5, 2019. www.wired.com.
5. Quoted in Dana Forsythe, "NYCC 2019: We Stepped Inside the Iron Man Suit in the New VR Game. It Was Wild," SYFY Wire, October 5, 2019. www.syfy.com.
6. VRROOM, "VR Games vs. Traditional Games: What's Best?," July 3, 2017. https://vrroom.buzz.
7. Quoted in Alan Bradley, "Does VR Have a Future, and What Does It Hold?," PC Gamer, March 2019. www.pcgamer.com.
8. Quoted in Bradley, "Does VR Have a Future, and What Does It Hold?"
9. Quoted in Bradley, "Does VR Have a Future, and What Does It Hold?"
10. Quoted in Bradley, "Does VR Have a Future, and What Does It Hold?"
11. Quoted in Charles Singletary, "Location-Based VR Gaming and the Biggest Obstacle VR Arcades Face," *Forbes*, July 25, 2019. www.forbes.com.
12. Malcolm Burt, "Virtual Reality Has Added a New Dimension to Theme Park Rides—So What's Next for Thrill-Seekers?," The Conversation, January 8, 2018. http://theconversation.com.
13. Quoted in Arthur Levine, "Virtual Reality: VR Tech Added to Theme Park Rides," WZZM13, June 20, 2018. www.wzzm13.com.

14. Quoted in Y-Jean Mun-Delsalle, "Artists Laurie Anderson and Hsin-Chien Huang Take Visitors on a Virtual Reality Voyage to the Moon," *Forbes*, April 23, 2019. www.forbes.com.
15. Quoted in Sol Rogers, "Filmmakers Are Embracing VR, but Are Audiences Ready for VR Feature Films?," *Forbes*, October 17, 2018. www.forbes.com.

Chapter Two: Health and Medicine

16. Quoted in UTSA Today, "UTSA Stems the Doctor Shortage with Virtual Reality," March 13, 2019. www.utsa.edu.
17. Quoted in Shelby Metzger, "College of Medicine Developing Virtual Reality Training Simulation," *The Lantern* (Ohio State University), September 18, 2019. www.thelantern.com.
18. Quoted in "Doctors Are Saving Lives with VR," KSDK, July 28, 2017. www.ksdk.com.
19. Quoted in Wilson Criscione, "Virtual Anatomy: Eyeing the Future, WSU Medical School Students Explore Virtual Reality," Inlander, November 28, 2018. www.inlander.com.
20. Quoted in University of Cambridge, "Virtual Reality Can Spot Navigation Problems in Early Alzheimer's Disease," Science-Daily, May 23, 2019. www.sciencedaily.com.
21. Quoted in *Canadian Healthcare Technology*, "Ottawa Hospital to Use 3D VR in Brain Surgery," July 10, 2019. www .canhealth.com.
22. Quoted in Rutgers Health, "Fun and Games," August 5, 2019. www.rutgers.edu.
23. Quoted in Alex Hogan, "Watch: Can Virtual Reality Transform Physical Therapy?," KQED Science, August 31, 2018. www .kqed.org.
24. Quoted in American Homefront Project, "Pentagon Will Expand Virtual Reality PTSD Treatment After Florida Program Success," CPR News, March 30, 2019. www.cpr.org.
25. Quoted in Megan Thielking, "Can Virtual Reality Boost Positive Feelings in Patients with Depression?," STAT, April 22, 2019. www.statnews.com.
26. Quoted in IFL Science, "Immersive Virtual Reality Could Help Treat Depression." www.iflscience.com.

27. Quoted in Amanda Pederson, "5 Ways VR Will Disrupt Our Health in the Future," MDDI Online, March 13, 2018. www .mddionline.com.

Chapter Three: Education

28. Quoted in Tim Hinchcliffe, "Unimersiv Educational VR Lets You Explore Ancient Sites, Travel to Space, or Board the *Titanic*," *The Sociable* (blog), April 4, 2017. https://sociable.co.
29. Quoted in Margaret Rhodes, "Forget the School Bus—the Most Magical Field Trip Is in VR," *Wired*, June 27, 2016. www .wired.com.
30. Quoted in Bradley, "Does VR Have a Future, and What Does It Hold?"
31. Quoted in *Arkenea* (blog), "16 Experts Predict the Future of Virtual Reality."
32. Quoted in Roberto Torres, "How a North Philly School Is Using Its New VR Lab," Technical.ly Philly, February 27, 2018. https://technical.ly.
33. Quoted in Torres, "How a North Philly School Is Using Its New VR Lab."
34. Quoted in Hinchcliffe, "Unimersiv Educational VR Lets You Explore Ancient Sites, Travel to Space, or Board the *Titanic*."
35. Quoted in Peter Holley, "Fordham University Business Students Have a New Tool to Prepare Them for the Boardrooms: Virtual Reality," *Washington Post*, November 12, 2019. www .washingtonpost.com.
36. Quoted in Nathan Rott, "'An Eye-Opener': Virtual Reality Shows Residents What Climate Change Could Do," NPR, November 24, 2019. www.npr.org.
37. Quoted in Susanne Krause, "Learning Vocabulary in VR," Medium, October 28, 2016. https://blog.cospaces.io.
38. Quoted in James Rohrbach, "How New Technologies Are Changing Language Learning, for Better and Worse," *Forbes*, May 10, 2018. www.forbes.com.
39. Quoted in Lehman College, "Practice Makes Perfect as Virtual Reality Helps Students Conquer Fear of Public Speaking," December 12, 2018. www.lehman.edu.
40. Quoted in Holley, "Fordham University Business Students Have a New Tool to Prepare Them for the Boardrooms."

41. Quoted in Will Wright, "How a VR Hub Can Help Displaced Coal Miners in Kentucky," *Government Technology*, December 6, 2019. www.govtech.com.

Chapter Four: In the Workplace

42. Quoted in Service Futures, "What Is the Potential of Virtual Reality in the Workplace?" www.servicefutures.com.
43. Quoted in Kristin Houser, "Walmart Used VR to Prepare Its Workers for Black Friday," *Futurism*, November 23, 2018. https://futurism.com.
44. Quoted in Yuki Noguchi, "Virtual Reality Goes to Work, Helping to Train Employees," *Morning Edition*, NPR, October 8, 2019. www.npr.org.
45. Quoted in Noguchi, "Virtual Reality Goes to Work, Helping to Train Employees."
46. Quoted in CBS News, "Companies Use VR to Train Employees for Hostage Situations, Robberies," December 20, 2018. www.cbsnews.com.
47. Quoted in ExxonMobil, "ExxonMobil Awards License to EON Reality for Immersive 3D Operator Training Simulator Technology," May 4, 2015. https://news.exxonmobil.com.
48. Quoted in Rolls-Royce, "Rolls-Royce and Qatar Airways Use Virtual Reality to Train Engineers," April 15, 2019. www.rolls-royce.com.
49. Quoted in Rolls-Royce, "Rolls-Royce and Qatar Airways Use Virtual Reality to Train Engineers."
50. Quoted in Rachel Lanham, "Can VR Elevate Your Restaurant's Training Program?," *QSR*, October 2019. www.qsrmagazine.com.
51. Quoted in Noguchi, "Virtual Reality Goes to Work, Helping to Train Employees."
52. Alexandra Berger, "The Future of Virtual Reality in the Workplace," HR Technologist, August 2, 2019. www.hrtechnologist.com.
53. Quoted in Bradley, "Does VR Have a Future, and What Does It Hold?"
54. Naveen Joshi, "Retailers Have a Lot to Gain from AR and VR," *Forbes*, October 1, 2019. www.forbes.com.

Chapter Five: Travel

55. Quoted in Betsy Mann, "Can Campus Tours in Virtual Reality Improve College Access?," EdSurge, April 1, 2019. www.edsurge.com.

56. Quoted in Mann, "Can Campus Tours in Virtual Reality Improve College Access?"

57. Quoted in Josh Moody, "How to Make the Most of Virtual College Tours," *U.S. News & World Report*, July 30, 2019. www.usnews.com.

58. Quoted in Moody, "How to Make the Most of Virtual College Tours."

59. Quoted in Curtis Silver, "How Virtual Reality Could Offer Vacations Without Leaving the House," *Vice*, August 30, 2016. www.vice.com.

60. Quoted in John Gaudiosi, "Royal Caribbean Is Embracing Internet of Things, Virtual Reality," AList, November 10, 2017. www.alistdaily.com.

61. Quoted in Marc Berman, "5 Real Uses of Virtual Reality in Education," Programming Insider, September 3, 2019. https://programminginsider.com.

62. Quoted in Kara Platoni, "Virtual Reality Aimed at the Elderly Finds New Fans," NPR, June 29, 2016. www.npr.org.

63. Sol Rogers, "Five Companies Using Virtual Reality to Improve the Lives of Senior Citizens," *Forbes*, August 21, 2019. www.forbes.com.

64. Quoted in Rogers, "Five Companies Using Virtual Reality to Improve the Lives of Senior Citizens."

65. Tobey Grumet Segal, "Virtual Reality Travel Experiences That Are Almost as Good as the Real Thing," Condé Nast Traveler, June 22, 2017. www.cntraveler.com.

66. Quoted in WCAX, "New Digital Spas Serve Up Virtual Vacations," August 14, 2019. www.wcax.com.

67. Quoted in *The Guardian* (Manchester), "Can Virtual Reality Emerge as a Tool for Conservation?," June 28, 2016. www.theguardian.com.

68. Quoted in *The Guardian* (Manchester), "Can Virtual Reality Emerge as a Tool for Conservation?"

69. Quoted in *Arkenea* (blog), "16 Experts Predict the Future of Virtual Reality."

Books

Samuel Greengard, *Virtual Reality*. Cambridge, MA: MIT Press, 2019.

Jaron Lanier, *Dawn of the New Everything: Encounters with Reality and Virtual Reality*. New York: Holt, 2017.

Paul Mealy, *Virtual and Augmented Reality for Dummies*. Hoboken, NJ: Wiley, 2018.

Carla Mooney, *What Is the Future of Virtual Reality?* San Diego, CA: ReferencePoint, 2017.

Erin Pangilinan, *Creating Augmented and Virtual Realities: Theory and Practice for Next-Generation Spatial Computing*. Sebastopol, CA: O'Reilly Media, 2019.

Michael Wohl, *The 360° Video Handbook: A Step-by-Step Guide to Creating Video for Virtual Reality (VR)*. Self-published, 2019.

Internet Sources

CNET, "Virtual Reality 101." www.cnet.com.

Franklin Institute, "The Science of Virtual Reality," 2019. www.fi.edu.

Bridget Poetker, "The Very Real History of Virtual Reality (+A Look Ahead)," Learning Hub, September 26, 2019. https://learn.g2.com.

Valentina Shin, "MIT Explains: How Does Virtual Reality Work," Khan Academy, 2020. www.khanacademy.org.

Websites

ClassVR (www.classvr.com). Find out how VR is being used in education and in a variety of career fields. This website has information about hundreds of VR apps for people interested in exploring science, the arts, history, and other subjects through virtual reality. Learn how other students are developing VR projects in the classroom.

How Virtual Reality Works, HowStuffWorks (https://electronics.howstuffworks.com/gadgets/other-gadgets/virtual-reality.htm). Learn about what goes into creating VR environments, how the headsets work, what is and is not possible with current VR technology, and where virtual reality and augmented reality are headed in the near future. Get a detailed but understandable explanation of the vocabulary of VR too.

Virtual Reality Society (www.vrs.org.uk). Get the latest news and reviews about VR apps and products, as well as information about how virtual reality is applied in sports, medicine, the arts, entertainment, and other fields. There is also information about some of the challenges of VR and some of the controversies and concerns about people spending more time in virtual worlds.

Virtual Reality, TechCrunch (https://techcrunch.com/virtual-reality-2). Read the latest news from all over the world about VR products and the business side of virtual reality. Learn who the leaders in the field are and what new games, apps, and other products are coming in the months ahead.

James Roland started out as a newspaper reporter more than twenty-five years ago. He then moved on to become an editor, magazine writer, and author.